NOSTALGIC VILLAGE

MANHATTAN

MW00736689

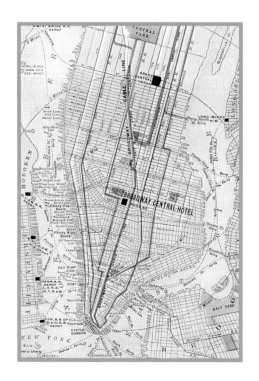

NOSTALGIC VIEWS OF
MANHATTAN

Copyright © 2005 by Jeff Hirsh
ISBN 1-58973-004-6

Library of Congress control number: 2005933189

Published by Arcadia Publishing for Borders Group, Inc.
Visit us on the internet at www.arcadiapublishing.com

CONTENTS

Introduction		7
1.	Between the Rivers	9
2.	Shopping and Transportation	29
3.	Commerce and Night Life	53
4.	Evolution of Skyscrapers	83
5.	Open Spaces	107

INTRODUCTION

Perhaps no city skyline in the world is as impressive as Manhattan's. Yet until the 1880s, no New York building stood taller than the spire of architect Richard Upjohn's Trinity Church. Horses pulled the trolleys, gas lamps lit the streets, and steam-powered elevated trains chugged north from the battery to upper Manhattan.

Then in 1883, John Augustus Roebling's Brooklyn Bridge was opened. The outlines of this incredible engineering feat could be seen rising above the island's eastern skyline. In a few years it was joined by the Statue of Liberty guarding the southern horizon. New Yorkers started looking *up*.

The bustling seaport was already the largest city in America, but it was rapidly running out of room to expand. Corporate America was growing fast and needed to house a swelling army of clerks and managers within the narrow confines of lower Manhattan. The evolution of skeletal steel construction technology in the 1880s ended reliance on load-bearing walls and lifted previous limits on the practical height of new buildings. The technology was born in Chicago but soared to new heights in Manhattan as it was done to excess here. A succession of technological advances, from electric lights and telephones to safe elevators, made skyscrapers feasible. Soon thousands of office workers did their jobs on relatively small footprints of land and by the turn of the century, there were more skyscrapers on the island than anywhere else in the world.

Manhattan rapidly grew into a world financial center and also became America's preeminent East Coast port. From the 1880s to the 1920s, an ever-increasing number of steamships delivered the very rich and, in far greater numbers, the very poor to the city's doors.

The former made the voyage on the palatial reaches of the steamships' upper decks. In Manhattan, they were the catalyst that spawned the gilded era of its office buildings, hotels, and restaurants.

The latter travelled deep below decks. From the damp, dark reaches of the steamers poured a flood of immigrant labor and talent that enriched Manhattan's industries. The flow of rich and poor generated a vast well of material drawn upon by writers and artists who chronicled the end of the nineteenth and beginning of the twentieth centuries.

This book presents a photographic record of these glorious decades of Manhattan's history, when the city embraced technology and immigration, and came of age.

ONE

BETWEEN THE RIVERS

A bird's-eye view of Manhattan in the 1890s shows Governor's Island (right foreground) and the Brooklyn Bridge dominating the skyline (right center).

Immigrant pushcart vendors
and shoppers crowd a street in
Manhattan's lower East Side, 1900.

OPPOSITE: New York Harbor
from the foot of Manhattan.
The aquarium, formerly Castle
Gardens, is at the lower left.
Before Ellis Island, this is where
many immigrants first entered the
country.

The 950-foot S.S. *Leviathan* approaching Manhattan. With accommodations for 3,700 passengers, it was the world's largest and probably the most luxurious steamship when it was launched in 1913.

Trains, trolleys, and horse carts on the Brooklyn Bridge.

OPPOSITE: The Manhattan Bridge in 1911.

Manhattan Bridge and East River, New York.

© 1911 BY GEO. P. HALL & SON N.Y.

21576

The Brooklyn Bridge in the 1890s, about a decade after its opening.

American Line Docks at the foot of Fulton Street.

East River wharves photographed from the Brooklyn Bridge.

The Chelsea Docks, about 1910.

Madison Square looking north in the early 1900s. The building on the far left is the Fifth Avenue Hotel.

TWO

SHOPPING
AND TRANSPORTATION

Double-decker buses at Madison Square.

A subway entrance in the first years of the twentieth century.

Shoppers and traffic on Twenty-Third Street around 1910.

Over time, the focus of shopping moved north to Herald Square.

Macy's new store opened in the early 1920s.

ESSEX BANNER.

THE MAMMOTH DRY GOODS STORE IN HAVERH
MACY'S

1853
Rowland H. Macy, a retired whaling skipper, opened a dry goods store in Haverhill, Massachusetts, and advertised that he would sell at lowest prices for cash.

1924
Still governed by the original policy which Rowland H. Macy boldly laid down, Greater Macy's has become the largest and busiest department store in New York.

OPPOSITE: R. H. Macy, the first store on Herald Square.

Traffic in the Bowery.

Fifth Avenue looking north from
Forty-Second Street.

OPPOSITE: Traffic on Fifth Avenue.

Sunday morning traffic on Fifth Avenue.

Early traffic in the Holland Tunnel.

OPPOSITE: The entrance to the tunnel.

For just a few years after the turn of the century, Fifth Avenue between Fiftieth and Fifty-Ninth Streets was able to maintain its quiet residential character.

By 1905, the motor car and "creeping commercialism" had changed everything.

Broadway looking north to Times Square.

Fifth Avenue at the turn of the twentieth century.

THREE

COMMERCE AND NIGHT LIFE

The ensemble of the Hollywood Cabaret Restaurant, Broadway at Forty-Eighth Street.

Hobble Skirt trolleys, introduced in 1914, had center doors built just inches from the ground to accommodate women in long skirts.

OPPOSITE: Broadway from Thirty-Third Street to Times Square, "The Great White Way," was the center for theater, hotels, and fine dining.

The New York Clearing House, 77 Cedar Street. In 1913 it handled transactions averaging nearly $324 million a day.

OPPOSITE: Curb brokers who dealt in the street. These were the predecessors of what would in 1953 become the American Stock Exchange. In 1921 the exchange moved indoors to 113 Greenwich Street.

City hall and City Hall Park. In the background are several of the buildings on Newspaper Row.

A horse-drawn pumper, captured on film as it sped to a fire.

Motor-propelled fire engines were introduced in 1907. By 1922 all horse-drawn vehicles in the city had been replaced.

The new Grand Central as it appeared in 1904.

Penn Station opened in 1910 at a cost of $100 million and connected New York and New Jersey via twin tunnels under the Hudson River.

Broadway at Astor Square. The Astor House hotel is on the left.

The Grand Union Hotel as it appeared just a few years before it was demolished in 1914 to make way for subway construction.

Hotel Astor on the left, looking north up Broadway and Seventh Avenue. The photograph was taken *c.* 1905 from the top of the Times Building.

A 1908 photograph of the large kitchen staff of the Knickerbocker.

An evening concert in the main foyer at the Waldorf-Astoria.

In its time, the Broadway Central was one of New York's finest hotels. The building began its checkered career as Tripler Hall in 1850, completed behind schedule, just slightly too late to house Jenny Lind's New York debut. The Swedish Nightingale did, however give 15 concerts there in the fall of that year. The building was remodeled and reopened in 1869 as the Grand Central Hotel. Robber baron Jim Fisk was ambushed and killed in the lobby in 1872 by Edward Stokes in a quarrel over the affections of actress Jessie Mansfield. In 1892 the hotel was renamed the Broadway Central and it met its end when an overhead crack gave way on August 3, 1973 and the hotel collapsed into a giant heap of rubble.

FOUR

EVOLUTION
OF SKYSCRAPERS

Until early in the 1890s, Trinity Church was the tallest structure in Manhattan.

By the time the photograph for this postcard was taken, Trinity Church was dwarfed by early-twentieth-century skyscrapers.

Steel cage construction, the technology that made the skyscraper feasible, is shown here at a turn-of-the-century construction site.

OPPOSITE: The Metropolitan Life Insurance Building's elevator and electrical machinery.

Sky Scraper in Course of Construction, New York.

George B. Post's 309-foot Pulitzer (World) Building, with its famed golden dome. It was the first building in New York City to rise above the steeple of Trinity Church. Its construction (1889–1890) marked the beginning of the wave of skyscraper construction that created what is now the Manhattan skyline.

OPPOSITE: Newspaper Row: the World Building, New York Sun, and the Tribune Building (1873–1875), designed by Richard Morris Hunt.

R. H. Robertson set a new height record (381 feet counting the tower) with his 30-story Park Row Building (1896–1899), also known as the Syndicate Building. The reported cost of the structure was $3.5 million.

OPPOSITE: The Equitable Building (1868–1870). Designed by Gilman and Kendall with George B. Post, it was just seven-and-a-half stories tall (shown here after it was destroyed by fire). It was the first Manhattan office building to include elevators in its design and was a precursor of the modern skyscraper.

The St. Paul Building, down the block and across the street from the Park Row Building.

The first of many exceptional Manhattan skyscrapers designed by Cass Gilbert, the Broadway and Chambers Building (1899–1900) is located across from City Hall Park. The tower is noted for its colorful brick and terra-cotta-clad facade. The smaller building to the left was the Shoe & Leather Bank.

The New York Times and Flat Iron buildings under construction. Skeletal steel construction used in these two buildings was still something of a novelty in the first years of the twentieth century. Many people were convinced that the Flat Iron Building would blow over in high winds.

Broadway looking toward the Times Building. In the distance is the Astor Hotel.

As the density of skyscrapers increased, loss of light and air became a widely recognized problem. Architect Ernest Flagg insisted that this would not be the case if a skyscraper occupied no more than 25 percent of its site, no matter what the building's height. To demonstrate this, he designed the Singer Tower (1906–1908), at the time the world's tallest building. Flagg's ideas ran into stiff opposition, but they were eventually incorporated into the city's revolutionary building code of 1916.

The Heckscher Building by Warren and Wetmore (1921) was the first skyscraper built under New York's innovative 1916 zoning law. The regulations mandated setbacks of upper stories that led to the "wedding cake" look. The Museum of Modern Art opened in 1929 in rented space in the Heckscher Building, which is now known as the Crown Building.

Women working in the Actuarial Division in the Metropolitan Life Insurance Building.

OPPOSITE: Over ten million records were stored on cards in this room in the Metropolitan Life Insurance Building.

The Woolworth Building, Cass Gilbert's Gothic masterpiece, seen through a graceful arch of the Municipal Building. From 1913 to 1930, the Woolworth reigned as the world's tallest building. A curtain wall of ivory-colored terra-cotta clothes the steel skeleton in a soaring array of flamboyant Gothic tracery that rises nearly 800 feet above street level.

OPPOSITE: The skyline looking east from the Woolworth Building.

The Williamsburg Bridge was the second span across the East River, built in hopes of relieving congestion on the Brooklyn Bridge, and was completed in December 1903. This photograph shows the approach at Delancy Street.

OPPOSITE: Heavy congestion at the Park Row entrance to the Brooklyn Bridge prior to completion of the East River Bridge.

The 1902 Flat Iron Building
was one of the early skyscrapers
built with the new steel beam
technology.

OPPOSITE: A 1905 motorized bus.
Within a few years after the turn
of the century, tourists were seeing
New York aboard motorized buses.
This one left from the recently
built Flat Iron Building.

FIVE

OPEN SPACES

An afternoon procession through Central Park at the turn of the twentieth century.

The swan pond in Central Park.

Gondoliers on the lake just after the turn of the twentieth century.

The lake and terrace.

The bandstand in Central Park.

Broadway at City Hall Park.

Madison Square with an open-air trolley.

Riverside Drive and the Columbia Yacht Club.

Immigrant station on Ellis Island. Between 1880 and 1905, well over 11 million people entered the country through Ellis Island.

Washington Square Park at night.